The ORIGIN of the RED CROSS

"Un Souvenir de Solferino"

BY

HENRI DUNANT

Translated from the French by
MRS. DAVID H. WRIGHT,
of the Philadelphia Chapter of the American
Red Cross, Independence Hall
Philadelphia, Pa.

1911
THE JOHN C. WINSTON CO.
PHILADELPHIA, PA.

Copyright, 1911,
By Mrs. David H. Wright.

JEAN HENRI DUNANT

PREFACE

Henri Dunant, the famous author of "A Souvenir of Solferino," was born in Geneva in 1828.

The instruction and philanthropic principles received by him in his youth, together with his natural energy and power of organization, were a good foundation for the unfolding of the ideas and inclinations which led to his fertile acts.

In 1859 occurred the event which definitely impelled him to a course of action which did not discontinue during his whole life. A course of action for the mitigation of the sufferings caused by war, or from a broader point of view, for the commencement of the reign of peace.

This event was the battle of Solferino, when he first organized, in Castiglione, corps of volunteers to search for and nurse the wounded.

Having thus started the idea of a permanent organization of these voluntary bands of compassionate workers, and also of an international treaty agreement in regard to the wounded, he presented himself

v

to *Marshal MacMahon and afterwards to Napoleon III, who became interested in the project of Dunant and immediately ordered his army no longer to make prisoners of the physicians and nurses of the enemy.*

Soon Dunant organized an Aid Committee in Geneva, and shortly afterwards he published his "Souvenir of Solferino," which was enthusiastically received and greatly applauded.

He met, however, opposition and obstacles, principally from the French Minister of War.

The philanthropic ideas of this book were received with interest by many European sovereigns with whom Dunant had intercourse, either by correspondence or by conversation; he always propagated persistently his ideas in regard to the organization of a national permanent committee for the wounded, his International Treaty, and the neutralization of those injured in war (he developed in separate works his ideas which were outlined only in the "Souvenir."

The Geneva Society of Public Utility created a commission for the purpose of studying the question. Meanwhile Dunant had the opportunity to speak with the King of Saxony, and to persuade representatives of some other countries to take up the question with their respective sovereigns.

Dunant interested the governments so much in his project that various nations sent delegates to the International Conference, which was held in Geneva, in 1863, when it was decided to establish a National Committee, and when the desire was expressed that the neutralization of the physicians, nurses and injured should be provided by treaty, and for the adoption of a distinctive and uniform international emblem and flag for the hospital corps, and the unanimous thanks of this Conference were extended to Dunant.

To consider this subject, a diplomatic International Congress was held in 1864, at Geneva, by invitation of the Swiss Federate Counsel. The treaty there drafted accepted the projects of Dunant and the formation of Volunteer Aid Societies, later called Red Cross Societies, was recommended by the Convention to the signatory powers.

In the further development of the ideas of Dunant The Hague Conference, in 1899, extended the provisions of the Treaty of Geneva to naval warfare.

Thus, a single individual, inspired with the sentiment of kindness and compassion for

*his fellow-creatures, by his own untiring
energy attained the realization of his ideas,
and aided in the progress of mankind toward
peace.*

*Thus, truly all men, and above all, the
workers for peace, owe to this laborer
merited and everlasting gratitude and re-
membrance.*

. . . . . .

The recompense, however, arrived late.

*In the zealous propaganda, for which, dur-
ing four years, he edited pamphlets and
articles in all languages, and traveled con-
tinuously through the whole of Europe,
Dunant spent everything that he possessed,
and, for many years, nothing more was
heard of the modest and good man, to whom
the approval of his conscience was all sufficient.*

*At last, in 1897, he was discovered in the
Swiss village of Heiden, where he was living
in misery, in a "Home" for old men, with
almost no means other than a small pension
received from the Empress of Russia.*

*The Baroness von Suttner sent at that
time to the press of the whole world, and
especially to those interested in International
Peace, an appeal to raise a contribution of
money to ease his last years. In 1901, when*

*the Nobel-Peace-Prize, valued at 208,000
francs, was awarded for the first time, it
was divided between Henri Dunant and
Frederick Passy.*

*It is true that many peace workers did
not approve of this decision of the Nobel
Committee. They said in opposition, that
the projects of Dunant not only were not
pacific, but could even have the contrary
effect. To lessen the terrors of war is really,
according to them, to destroy the most effective means of turning men from it, and
consequently tended to prolong the duration
of its reign. One of the chief representatives
of this idea, Signor H. H. Fried, said that
the Geneva Convention was only a small
concession by the governments to the new
idea that is fighting against war.*

*Without doubt, they do not approve of the
humane plan of Dunant, on the contrary,
they think that it is not essentially peace-
making; that it should not be recompensed
by the first peace prize, and that it is dangerous to confuse pacification with simple hu-
manitarianism.*

*The contrary opinion is shown by the fol-
lowing words, written by Signor Ruyssin,
in the review "Peace by Right," at the time
when Dunant received his prize:*

"His glory has grown each year in proportion to all the lessening of suffering which his work has accomplished, to all the lives which it saves, and to all the self-devotion to which it gives birth.

"Henri Dunant has decreased the abomination of war; Frederick Passy fought to make it impossible. One has accomplished more; the other has created more remote, but brighter hopes. One has harvested already; the other sows for the future harvest; and so it would be arbitrary and unjust to compare such dissimilar lines of work, both equally meritorious. The accomplishment of the wishes of Nobel rightly placed identical crowns on the heads of two old men who employed their lives in fighting against war."

This disagreement is interesting in that it shows the contrary judgment to which different zealous peace workers were led in regard to the project of Dunant.

Whatever may be the conclusion of the reader, about the relation between it and the peace propaganda, he will certainly be of the opinion that "A Souvenir of Solferino," showing the abominations of war, is a useful instrument of the propaganda, and that the name of Dunant should be blessed, as

*that of one of the most self-devoted bene-
factors of mankind.*

*Henri Dunant died at Heiden, Switzer-
land, on October the thirty-first, 1910.*

THE ORIGIN OF THE RED CROSS

The bloody victory of Magenta opened the gates of Milan to the French Army, which the towns of Pavia, Lodi and Cremona welcomed enthusiastically.

The Austrians, abandoning the lines of the Adda, the Oglio, and the Chiese, gathered their forces on the bank of the River Mincio, at whose head the young and courageous Emperor Joseph placed himself.

The King of Sardinia, Victor Emmanuel, arrived on the seventeenth of June, 1859, at Brescia, where, with great joy, the inhabitants welcomed him, seeing in the son of Charles Albert a saviour and a hero. During the next day the French Emperor entered the same town amid the enthusiastic cries of the people, happy to show their gratitude to the monarch who came to help them gain their independence.

On the twenty-first of June, Napoleon III and Victor Emmanuel II left Brescia, from which place their armies had departed during the previous day. On the twenty-second they occupied Lonato, Castenedolo and Montechiaro. On the evening of the twenty-third Napoleon, who was commander-in-chief, published strict orders for the army of the King of Sardinia, encamped at Desenzano, and forming the left flank of the allied armies, to proceed early the following day to Pozzelengo.

Marshal Baraguey d' Hilliers was ordered to march on Solferino; Marshal MacMahon, Duke de Magenta, on Cavriana; General Neil was to proceed to Guidizzolo; Marshal Canrobert to Medole; Marshal Regnaud de Saint-Jean d' Angley, with the Imperial Guard, to Castiglione.

These united forces amounted to 150,000 men, with 400 cannon.

The Austrian Emperor had at his disposition, in the Lombardo-Venetian kingdom, nine army corps, amounting in all to 250,000 men, comprising the garrison of Verona and Mantua. The effective force prepared to enter the line of battle consisted of seven corps, some 170,000 men, supported by 500 cannon.

The headquarters of the Emperor Francis Joseph had been moved from Verona to Villafranca, then to Valeggio. On the evening of the twenty-third the Austrian troops received the order to recross the River Mincio during the night to Peschiera, Salionze, Valeggio, Ferri, Goito and Mantua. The main part of the army took up its position from Pozzolengo to Guidizzolo, in order to attack the enemy between the Rivers Mincio and Chiese.

The Austrian forces formed two armies. The first having as Commander-in-chief Count Wimpffen, under whose orders were the corps commanded by Field Marshals Prince Edmund Schwarzenberg, Count Schaffgotsche and Baron Veigl, also the cavalry division of Count Zeidewitz. This composed the left flank. It was stationed in the neighborhood of Volta, Guidizzolo, Medole and Castel-Gioffredo.

The second army was commanded by Count Schlick, having under his orders the Field Marshals Count Clam-Gallas, Count Stadion, Baron Zobel and Cavalier Benedek, as well as the cavalry division of Count Mensdorf. This composed the right flank. It occupied Cavriana, Pozzolengo and San Martino.

Thus, on the morning of the twenty-fourth, the Austrians occupied all the heights between Pozzolengo, Solferino, Cavriana and Guidizzolo. They ranged their artillery in series of breastworks, forming the center of the attacking line, which permitted their right and left flanks to fall back upon these fortified heights which they believed to be unconquerable.

The two belligerent armies, although marching one against the other, did not expect such a sudden meeting. Austria, misinformed, supposed that only a part of the allied army had crossed the Chiese River. On their side the confederates did not expect this attack in return, and did not believe that they would find themselves so soon before the army of the Austrian Emperor. The reconnoitering, the observations and the reports of the scouts, and those made from the fire balloons during the day of the twenty-third showed no signs of such an imminent encounter.

The collision of the armies of Austria and Franco-Sardinia on Friday, the twenty-fourth of June, 1859, was, therefore, unexpected, although the combatants on both sides conjectured that a great battle was near.

The Austrian army, already fatigued by the difficult march during the night of the twenty-third and twenty-fourth, had to support from the earliest dawn the attack of the enemies' armies and to suffer from the

4

intensely hot weather as well as from hunger and thirst, for, except a double ration of brandy, the greater number of the Austrians were unable to take any food.

The French troops already in movement before daybreak had had nothing but coffee. Therefore, this exhaustion of the soldiers, and above all, of the unfortunate wounded, was extreme at the end of this very bloody battle, which lasted more than fifteen hours.

Both armies are awake.

Three hundred thousand men are standing face to face. The line of battle is ten miles long.

Already at three o'clock in the morning, corps commanded by Marshals Baraguey d' Hilliers and MacMahon are commencing to move on Solferino and Cavriana.

Hardly have the advance columns passed Castiglione when they themselves are in the presence of the first posts of the Austrians, who dispute the ground.

On all sides bugles are playing the charges and the drums are sounding.

The Emperor Napoleon who passed the night at Montechiaro hastens rapidly to Castiglione.

By six o'clock a furious fire has commenced.

The Austrians march in a compact mass in perfect order along the open roads. In the air are flying their black and yellow standards, on which are embroidered the ancient Imperial arms.

The day is very clear. The Italian sun makes the brilliant equipments of the dragoons, the lancers and the cuirassiers of the French army glitter brightly.

At the commencement of the engagement the Emperor Francis Joseph, together with his entire staff, leaves headquarters in order to go to Volta. He is accompanied by the Archdukes of the House of Lorraine, among whom are the Grand Duke of Tuscany and the Duke of Modena.

In the midst of the difficulties of a field unknown to the French army the first meeting takes place. It has to make its way through plantations of mulberry trees, interlaced by climbing vines, which form almost impassable barriers.

The earth is cut by great dried up trenches which the horses have to leap, and by long walls with broad foundations which they have to climb.

From the hills the Austrians pour on the enemy a constant hail of shot and shell. With the smoke of the cannon's continual discharge the rain of bullets is ploughing up the earth and dust into thousands of missiles.

The French hurl themselves upon these strongly fortified places in spite of the firing of the batteries which falls upon the earth with redoubled force.

During the burning heat of noon the battle everywhere becomes more and more furious.

Column after column throw themselves one against the other with the force of a devastating torrent.

A number of French regiments surround masses of Austrian troops, but, like iron walls, these resist and at first remain unshaken.

Entire divisions throw their knapsacks to the earth in order to rush at the enemy with fixed bayonets.

If a battalion is driven away another replaces it; each hill, each height, each rocky eminence becomes a theatre for an obstinate struggle.

On the heights, as well as in the ravines, the dead lie piled up. The Austrians and the allied armies march one against the other, killing each other above the blood-covered corpses, butchering with gunshots, crushing each other's skulls or disemboweling with the sword or bayonet. No cessation in the

7

conflict, no quarter given. The wounded are defending themselves to the last. It is butchery by madmen drunk with blood.

Sometimes the fighting becomes more terrible on account of the arrival of rushing, galloping cavalry. The horses, more compassionate than their riders, seek in vain to step over the victims of this butchery, but their iron hoofs crush the dead and dying. With the neighing of the horses are mingled blasphemies, cries of rage, shrieks of pain and despair.

The artillery, at full speed, follows the cavalry which has cut a way through the corpses and the wounded lying in confusion on the ground. A jaw-bone of one of these last is torn away; the head of another is battered in; the breast of a third is crushed. Limbs are broken and bruised; the field is covered with human remains; the earth is soaked with blood.

The French troops, with fiery ardor, scale the steep hills and rocky declivities in spite of shot and shell.

Hardly does some harassed and profusely perspiring company capture a hill and reach its summit, when it falls like an avalanche on the Austrians, overthrows, repulses and pursues them to the depths of the hollows.

8

But the Austrians regain the advantage. Ambuscaded behind the houses, the churches and the walls of Medole, Solferino and Cavriana, they heroically fight on and very nearly win the victory.

The unending combat rages incessantly and in every place with fury. Nothing stops, nothing interrupts the butchery. They are killing one another by the hundreds. Every foot of ground is carried at the bayonet's point, every post disputed foot by foot. From the hands of the enemy are taken villages, house after house, farm after farm, each is the theatre of a siege. Doors, windows and courts are abattoirs.

A rain of cannon balls is sending death to the distant reserves of Austria. If these desert the field they yield it only step by step, and soon recommence action. Their ranks are ceaselessly reforming. On the plains the wind raises the dust, which flies over the roads like dense clouds, darkening the day and blinding the fighters.

The French cavalry flings itself on the Austrian cavalry; uhlans and hussars slash furiously at each other with their swords.

The rage is so great that in some places, after the exhaustion of the cartridges and

9

the breaking of the muskets, they fight with fists and beat one another with stones.

The strongest positions are captured, lost, and recaptured, to be lost again. Everywhere men are falling mutilated, riddled with bullets, covered with wounds.

In the midst of these endless combats, these massacres, blasphemies arise in different tongues, telling of the diverse nationalities of the men, many of whom are obliged to become homicides in their twentieth year.

The soldiers of the Sardinian King, defending and attacking with fervor, continue their skirmishes from early morning. The hills of San Martino, Roccolo, Madonno della Scoperta are captured and recaptured five or six times. Their Generals Mollard, La Marmora, Della Rocca, Durando, Fanti, Cialdini, Cucchiari, de Sonnoz, with all kinds and all grades of officers help the king before whose eyes lie the wounded Generals Cedale, Perrier and Arnoldi.

The French Emperor orders that the corps of Baraguey d' Hilliers and MacMahon, together with the Imperial Guard, attack at the same time the fortress of San Cassiano and occupy Solferino.

But the brave Austrians make the allied army pay dearly for its success. . . . .

10

One of its heroes, Prince Aleksandro de Hessen, after fighting with great courage at San Cassiano defends against repeated attacks, the three heights of Mount Fontana. . . . . At Guidizzolo, Prince Charles of Windischraetz, braves certain death in seeking to recapture under a hail of balls Casa Nova. Mortally wounded, he still commands, supported and carried by his brave soldiers, who vainly make for him a rampart of their own bodies.

Marshal Baraguey d' Hilliers finally enters the town of Solferino, courageously defended by Baron Stadion.

The sky is darkened, dense clouds cover the horizon. A furious wind is rising. It carries away the broken branches of the trees. A cold rain, driven by the tempest, a veritable cloud-burst, drenches the combatants, exhausted from hunger and fatigue, while dust, hail and smoke are blinding the soldiers forced to fight also the elements.

The army of the Emperor Francis Joseph retreats. Throughout the entire action the chief of the House of Hapsburg shows admirable tranquillity and self-control.

During the capture of Cavriana the Austrian Emperor finds himself, together with Baron Schlick and the Prince of Nassau, on

11

the adjacent heights, Madonna della Pieve, opposite a church surrounded by cypress trees. Towards evening, the Austrian center having yielded and the left flank not daring to hope to force the position of the allies, the general retreat is decided. In this grave moment, Emperor Francis Joseph, around whom rained balls and bullets during the whole day, goes with a part of his staff to Volta, while the Archdukes and the hereditary Grand Duke of Tuscany returned to Valeggio.

The Austrian officers fought like lions. Some, through despair, let themselves die, but sold their lives dearly. The greater number rejoin their regiments covered with the blood of their own wounds or with that of the enemy. To their bravery should be rendered merited praise.

. . . . Guidizzolo remains occupied by the Austrians until ten o'clock in the evening. . . . . The roads are covered with army wagons, carts and reserve artillery. The transport vans are saved by the rapid construction of improvised bridges. The first Austrian wounded consisting of men slightly injured, commence to enter Villafranca. The more seriously wounded follow them. Austrian physicians and their assistants rapidly bandage the wounds, give some nourishment to the wounded and send them by railroad trains to Verona, where the embarrassment is becoming terrible.

Although during its retreat the Austrian army tries to carry away all the wounded which it could transport (and with what great suffering!), nevertheless, thousands remain lying on the ground moistened with their blood.

The allied army is in possession of the conquered field.

Near the close of the day when the evening shadows creep over this vast field of carnage, more than one officer, more than one French soldier, seek here and there a comrade, a compatriot, or a friend, when he finds the wounded friend, he kneels beside, trying to restore him to consciousness, wiping away the blood, bandaging the wounds as well as he can, wrapping a handkerchief around the broken limb, but rarely can he secure water for the suffering man.

How many silent tears were shed during this sad night, when all false pride, all human regard were set aside.

During the battle, hospitals for the wounded established in nearby farmhouses, churches, monasteries, in the open air, under

13

the shade of trees receive the wounded officers and non-commissioned officers, who are hastily given treatment. After these comes the turn of the soldiers, when that is possible. Those of the latter who are still able to walk find their way to the field hospitals. The others are carried on litters and stretchers, weakened as they are by loss of blood, by pain, by continued lack of food, and by the mental and moral shock they have experienced. During the battle a pennant fixed on an elevation marks the station for the wounded and the field hospitals of the fighting regiments. Unfortunately, only a few of the soldiers know the color of the hospital pennant or that of the hospital flag of the enemy, for the colors differ with the different nations. The bombs fall upon them, sparing neither physicians, nor wounded, nor wagons loaded with bread, wine, meat or lint.

The heights which extend from Castiglione to Volta, sparkle with thousands of fires, which are fed by pieces of Austrian gun-wagons and by huge branches of trees, broken by the tempest or by cannon balls. The soldiers dry their dripping clothes; then, overcome by fatigue and exhaustion, they fall asleep on the stones or on the ground.

What terrible episodes! What touching scenes! What disillusionments!

There are battalions without food, companies lacking almost every necessity, because of the loss of the knapsacks. Water also is lacking, but their thirst is so intense that officers and soldiers resort to slimy and even bloody pools. Everywhere the wounded are begging for water.

Through the silence of the night are heard groans, stifled cries of anguish and pain, and heartrending voices calling for help.

Who will ever be able to paint the agonies of this horrible night!

The sun on the twenty-fifth of June, 1859, shines above one of the most frightful sights imaginable. The battlefield is everywhere covered with corpses of men and horses. They appear as if sown along the roads, in the hollows, the thickets and the fields, above all, near the village of Solferino.

The fields ready for the harvest are ruined, the grain trodden down, the fences overturned, the orchards destroyed.

Here and there one finds pools of blood.

The villages are deserted. They bear traces of bullets, of bombs and shells and grenades.

The houses whose walls have been pierced

15

with bullets and are gaping widely, are shaken and ruined.

The inhabitants, of whom the greater number have passed almost twenty hours in the refuge of their cellars, without light or food, are commencing to come out. The look of stupor of these poor peasants bears testimony to the long terror they have endured.

The ground is covered with all kinds of debris, broken pieces of arms, articles of equipments and blood-stained clothing.

The miserable wounded gathered up during the day are pale, livid and inert.

Some, principally those seriously injured, have a vacant look, they seem not to understand what is said to them. They turn their staring eyes toward those who bring them help.

Others, in a dangerous state of nervous shock, are shaking with convulsive tremblings.

Still others, with uncovered wounds, where inflammation has already appeared, seem frenzied with pain; they beg that some one may end their sufferings, and, with drawn faces, writhe in the last torments of agony.

Elsewhere, poor fellows are prostrated on the ground by bullets and bursting shells.

Their arms and legs have been fractured by the cannon wheels that have passed over them.

The shock of the cylindrical ball shatters the bones, so that the wound it causes is always very dangerous. The bursting of shells and the conical balls make extremely painful fractures, the internal injury being terrible. Every kind of pieces of bone, of earth, of lead, of clothing, of equipments, of shoes, aggravate and irritate the wounds of the patients and increase their sufferings.

Those who cross this vast field of yesterday's battle meet at every step, in the midst of a confusion without parallel, inexpressible despair and suffering of every kind.

Some of the battalions which had taken off their knapsacks during the battle, at last find them again, but they have been robbed of all their contents. During the night, vagabonds have stolen everything. A grave loss to the poor men whose linen and uniforms are stained and torn. Not only do they find themselves deprived of their clothing, but even their smallest savings, all their fortune as well as of the treasures dear to them; small family mementoes given by mothers, sisters and sweethearts.

In several places the dead are stripped of

17

their clothing by the thieves, who do not always spare the wounded who are still living.

Besides these painful sights are others still more dramatic.

Here the old, retired General Le Breton wanders, seeking his son-in-law, the wounded General Douay, who has left his daughter, Madame Douay, in the midst of the tumult of war, in a state of the most cruel uneasiness. There, Colonel de Maleville, shot at Casa Nova, expires. Here, it is Colonel de Genlis, whose dangerous wound causes a burning fever. There, Lieutenant de Selve of the artillery, only a few weeks out of Saint Cyr, has his right arm amputated on the battlefield, where he was wounded.

I help care for a poor sergeant-major of the Vincennes Chasseurs, both of whose legs are pierced through with balls. I meet him again in the Brescia Hospital; but he will die crossing Mount Cenis.

Lieutenant de Guiseul, who was believed dead, is picked up on the spot, where, having fallen with his standard, he was lying in a swoon. The courageous sub-lieutenant Fournier, of the flying-guard, gravely wounded, finishes in his twentieth year a military career commenced in his tenth year by voluntarily enlisting in the foreign legion. They bury the Commander de Pontgibaud, who died during the night, and the young Count de Saint Paer, who had attained the rank of major hardly seven days before. General Auger, of the artillery, is carried to the field hospital of Casa Morino. His left shoulder has been shattered by a six-inch shell, part of which remained imbedded for twenty-four hours in the interior of the muscles of the armpit. Carried to Castiglione he is attacked with gangrene, and dies as a result of the disarticulation of the arm. General de Ladmirault and General Dieu, both gravely wounded, also arrived at Castiglione.

The lack of water becomes greater and greater. The sun is burning, the ditches are dried up. The soldiers have only brackish and unwholesome water to appease their thirst. Where even the least little stream or spring trickling drop by drop is found, guards with loaded guns have great difficulty in preserving this water for the most urgent needs.

Wounded horses, who have lost their riders, and have wandered during the whole night, drag themselves to their comrades, from whom they seem to beg for help. They

19

are put out of their agony by a bullet. One of these noble chargers comes alone into the midst of a French company. The rich saddle-bag, fastened to the saddle, shows that it belongs to Prince von Isenberg. Afterwards, the wounded Prince himself is found; but careful nursing during a serious illness will allow him to return to Germany, where his family, in ignorance of the truth, have believed him dead and have mourned for him.

Among the dead some have peaceful faces; these are the men who were struck suddenly and died at once. But those who did not perish immediately have their limbs rigid and twisted in agony, their bodies are covered with dirt; their hands clutch the earth, their eyes are open and staring, a convulsive contraction has uncovered their clenched teeth.

Three days and three nights are passed in burying the dead who are left on the battle-field.

On so large a field, many of the corpses hidden in the ditches, covered by the thickets or by some uneveness of the ground are discovered very late. They, as well as the dead horses, emit a fetid stench.

In the French army a number of soldiers from each company are detailed to recognize

and bury the dead. As far as possible soldiers of the same corps must pick up their
fellow-members. They write down the number stamped on the clothing of the dead.
Then, aided in this painful duty by paid
Lombardy peasants, they put the corpses in
a common grave. Unfortunately, it is possible that, because of the unavoidable rapid-
ity in this labor, and because of the careless-
ness and inattention of the paid workmen,
more than one living man is buried with the
dead.

The letters, papers, orders, money,
watches found on the officers are sent to
their families, but the great number of the
interred bodies make the faithful accomplishment of this task impossible.

A son, the idol of his parents, educated
and cared for during many years by a lov-
ing mother who was uneasy at the very
slightest indisposition. A brilliant officer,
beloved by his family, having left at home
his wife and children. A young soldier who
has just left his betrothed and his mother,
sisters and old father; there he lies in the
mud and in the dust, soaked in his own blood.
Because of the wound in his head his face
has become unrecognizable. He is in agony,
he expires in cruel suffering, and his body,

21

black, swollen, hideous, thrown in a shallow
grave, is covered with a little lime and earth.
The birds of prey will not respect his feet
and hands protruding from the muddy
ground of the slope which serves him as a
tomb. Some one will come back, will carry
more earth there and, perhaps, will put up
a wooden cross above the place where his
body rests, and that will be all.

The corpses of the Austrians, clothed in
mud-stained cloaks, torn linen jackets, white
tunics stained with blood are strewn by
thousands on the hills and plains of Medole.
Clouds of crows fly over the bodies in hopes
of having them for prey.

By hundreds they are crowded into a great
common grave.

Once out of the line of fire, Austrian soldiers, slightly wounded, young first-year re-
cruits, throw themselves on the ground from
fatigue and inanition, then weakened by
loss of blood, they die miserably from exhaustion and hunger.

Unhappy mothers in Austria, Hungary
and Bohemia, your sorrow will be great
when you learn that your children died in
the enemy's country, without care, without
help, and without consolation!

The lot of the Austrian prisoners-of-war

is very sad. Led like simple cattle, they are sent in a crowd, with a strong guard, to Brescia, where they at last find repose, if not a kind welcome.

Some French soldiers wish to do violence to the Hungarian captives whom they take for Croates, adding furiously that those "Glued-pantalooners," as they called them, always killed the wounded. I succeeded in tearing from their hands these unfortunate, trembling captives.

On the battle-field many Austrians are permitted to keep their swords. They have the same food as the French officers. Some troops of the allied army fraternally divide their biscuits with the famished prisoners. Some even take the wounded on their backs and carry them to the ambulances. Near me the lieutenant of the guard bandages with his white handkerchief the head of a Tyrolese which was scarcely covered with old, torn, and dirty linen.

During the previous day at the height of the battle, Commandant de la Rochefoucauld-Liancourt, the fearless African hunter, threw himself upon a squad of Hungarians; but his horse having been pierced through with balls, he himself was struck by two shots and made prisoner by the Hungarians.

23

Learning that wounded La Rochefoucauld had been captured by the soldiers, the Austrian Emperor ordered that he be treated with great kindness and given the best care.

The commissary continue to pick up the wounded. These, bandaged or not, are carried by mules or wheelbarrows and litters to the field hospitals in the villages and towns near the place where they fell.

In these towns, churches, monasteries, houses, parks, courts, streets and promenades are transformed into improvised hospitals.

In Carpenedolo, Castel-Goffredo, Medole, Guidizzolo, Volta and neighboring places are arriving many of the wounded. But the greater number are carried to Castiglione, where the least mutilated have already succeeded in dragging themselves.

Behold the long procession of vehicles of the Commissary Department, loaded with soldiers, non-commissioned officers and officers of all grades mixed together; cavalrymen, infantry, artillerymen, bleeding, fatigued, lacerated, covered with dust. Each jolt of the wagons which carry them imposing on them new suffering.

Then the mules come trotting in, their gait drawing, each instant, bitter cries from the throats of the unfortunate wounded whom they are bearing.

Many die during the transportation.

Their corpses are put on the sides of the roads. To others is left the duty of burying them. These dead are enscribed, "Disappeared."

The wounded are sent to Castiglione. From there they are carried on to the hospitals in Brescia, Cremona, Bergama, Milan, and other cities of Lombardy, where they will receive the regular care and will submit to the necessary amputations. But as the means of transportation are very scarce, they are obliged to wait several days in Castiglione. This city, where the confusion surpasses all imagination, soon becomes for the French and Austrians a vast temporary hospital.

On the day of battle the field-hospital of headquarters is established there. Chests of lint are unpacked, dressings for wounds and medicate necessities are prepared. The inhabitants give everything that they can get ready—coverings, linens, mattresses and straw.

The Hospital of Castiglione, the monastary, the Barracks of San Luigi, the Church of the Capucines, the stations of the police, the churches of Maggiore, San Giuseppe, Santa Rosalie, are filled with the wounded lying crowded on the straw.

Straw is also arranged for them in the courts and in the public parks. Plank roofs are quickly put up and linen is stretched to protect them from the hot sun.

The private dwellings are soon converted into hospitals. Officers and soldiers are there received by the inhabitants.

Some of these last run through the streets anxiously searching for a physician for their guests. Later, others, in consternation, go and come through the city, insistently begging that some one take away from their houses the corpses with which they do not know what to do.

A number of French surgeons, having remained in Castiglione, aided by young Italian physicians and by hospital orderlies, dress and bandage the wounds.

But all this is very insufficient.

The number of convoys of wounded becomes so great during Saturday that the administration, the citizens and the few soldiers left in Castiglione are incapable of caring for so much misery.

Then, melancholy scenes occur. There is water; there is food; and nevertheless the wounded are dying of hunger and thirst. There is much lint, but not enough hands to put it on the wounds! The greater number of the army of physicians must go to Cavriana; the hospital orderlies make mistakes, and hands are lacking at this critical moment.

A voluntary service, good or bad, must be organized. But this is difficult in the midst of such disorder, to which is added a panic of the Castiglionians, which results in aggravating the misery of the wounded. This panic is caused by a very insignificant circumstance.

As each corps of the French army had recovered itself, after taking up its position, on the day after the battle, convoys of prisoners were formed who were sent to Brescia, through Castiglione and Montechiaro. The inhabitants took one band of captives coming from Cavriana escorted by hussars, for the Austrian army returning in force. Alarm was given by the frightened peasants, by the assistant conductors of the baggage, by itinerant merchants who follow the troops in a campaign.

Immediately all the houses are closed, the inhabitants barricading themselves in their homes, burning the tri-color flags which had

27

adorned their windows, hiding themselves in the cellars or the attics. Some run into the fields with their wives and children carrying with them their most valuable possessions. Others, less frightened and more sagacious, remain at home, but take in the first Austrian wounded upon whom they lay their hands and overwhelm them with kindness and care.

In the streets, on the roads, blocked by wagonloads of wounded, by convoys of supplies, are rapid transport wagons, horses flying in all directions, amid cries of fear, of anger and of pain. Baggage wagons are overturned, bread and biscuits fall into the gutter. The drivers detach the horses, dashing away with hanging bridles on the road to Brescia, spreading the alarm as they go. They collide with carts of provisions and convoys of wounded. These latter, trodden under foot and frenzied with terror, beg to be taken with them. In the city some of them deaf to all orders tear away their bandages, go staggering out of the churches, into the streets where they are jostled and bruised and finally fall from exhaustion and pain.

What agonies! What suffering during the

28

days of June twenty-fifth, twenty-sixth and twenty-seventh!

Wounds poisoned by heat, by dust and by lack of water and care, have become intensely painful.

Suffocating stenches pollute the air in spite of efforts to keep in good condition these local hospitals.

Every quarter of an hour the convoys sent to Castiglione are bringing new loads of wounded. The insufficiency in the number of assistants, of hospital orderlies, of servants is cruelly felt.

In spite of the activity of the Commissary Department, which is organizing transportation to Brescia by means of ox-carts; in spite of the spontaneous care of the inhabitants of Castiglione, who transport the sick, the departures are much less numerous than the arrivals, and the crowding grows unceasingly greater.

On the stone floors of the churches of Castiglione are placed, side by side, men of every nation. French, Germans, Slavs and Arabs are temporarily crowded to the most remote part of the chapels. Many have no longer the strength to move themselves and cannot move or stir in the narrow space where they are lying. Oaths, blasphemies and cries which can be interpreted by no expression, are sounding beneath the arches of the sanctuaries.

"Ah, sir, how I suffer!" say to me some of these poor fellows. "We are abandoned, left to die miserably, and yet we fought bravely!" They can get no rest, in spite of the nights they have passed in sleeplessness and long-endured fatigue. In their distress they beg for help which is not given. Some, in despair, roll in convulsions which will end in tetanus and death. Others, believing that the cold water poured on their festered wounds produce worms, which appear in great numbers, refuse to have the bandages moistened. Others still, whose wounds were dressed at the improvised hospitals on the battle-fields, are given no further attention during the halt they are obliged to make in Castiglione, and as these bandages are very tight, in view of the roughness of the transportation and have not been changed, they are suffering veritable tortures.

These, whose faces are black with flies, with which the air is infested and which cling to their wounds, cast on all sides distracted glances. But no one notices. On these, the cloaks, shirts, flesh and blood form a compact mass that cannot be removed.

Here, lies a soldier totally disfigured; his tongue hanging far out of his broken jaws. He stirs and wishes to rise. I moisten his dried palate and hardened tongue. Seizing a handful of lint I soak it in a bucket and squeeze the water from this improvised sponge in the formless opening which is in the place of his mouth.

There, is an unfortunate man a part of whose face, the nose, lips and chin have been cut away by the stroke of a sword. Incapable of speech, half blind, he makes signs with his hands, and by that heartrending pantomime, accompanied by guttural sounds, draws attention to himself. I give him a drink by dropping gently on his blood-covered face a little pure water.

A third, with a cleft head, expires, his blood spreading over the stone floor of the church. He presents a horrible sight. His companions in misfortune push him with their feet, for he incommodes the passage. I protect his last moments and cover with a handkerchief his poor head which he still feebly moves.

Although every house has become an infirmary, and every family has dedicated itself to nursing the wounded officers, that it has gathered in, nevertheless I succeed by

Sunday morning in collecting a certain number of women of the people, who assist, as best they can, in the efforts made to help so many thousands of wounded men who are without succor. Food must be given, and above all, drink, to the men who literally are dying from hunger and thirst. Wounds must be bandaged, blood-stained bodies, covered all over with dirt and vermin, must be washed, and all this must be done in the extremely hot weather, in the midst of the suffocating, nauseating stench, and of groans and cries of pain.

Nevertheless, a little group of volunteers is formed. I organize, well as I can, aid in the section which seems to be the most without care, and I choose one of the churches of Castiglione, called Chiesa Maggiore.

Nearly five hundred soldiers are crowded together on the straw, about one hundred others, suffering and groaning, are lying in the public park before the church.

In the church the women of Lombardy go from one to the other with jars and pitchers full of clear water, which serves to appease the thirst and to bathe the wounds. Some of these improvised nurses are good-hearted old women, others are charming young girls. Their gentleness, goodness, compassion, and

their attentive care restores a little courage
to the wounded.

The boys of the neighborhood come and
go between the church and the nearby
springs with buckets, pitchers and jars.

The distribution of water is followed by
that of bouillon and soup, of which the servants of the Commissary Department are
obliged to cook a marvelous quantity.

Thick bundles of lint are placed here and
there. Every one can use it freely; but
bandages, linen and shirts are lacking, and
one can hardly procure the most necessary
articles. I purchase, however, some new
shirts by the aid of those kind-hearted
women who have already given all their old
linen; and, on Monday, early in the morning, I send my coachman to Brescia to bring
back supplies. He returns after some hours
with his cabriolet loaded with sponges, linen,
pins, cigars, tobacco, camomile, mallow, sam-
buca, oranges, sugar and lemons.

This makes it possible to give refreshing
lemonade, wash the wounds with mallow-
water, put on warm compresses and renew
the material of the bandages.

In the meantime we have gained some re-
cruits, who help us. The first is an old naval
officer, then some English tourists, who, de-

siring to see everything, have entered the church, and whom we keep almost by force. Two other Englishmen, on the contrary, show themselves desirous to help. They distribute cigars to the Austrians. An Italian priest, three or four travelers, a Swiss merchant from Neuchatel, a Parisian journalist, who afterwards takes charge of the relief in the adjacent church, and some officers whose company has received orders to remain in Castiglione, also aid us.

But soon some of those voluntary nurses go away, not being able to bear the sight of this suffering. The priest follows their example, but he reappears, however, with delicate kindness to make us smell aromatic herbs and bottles of salts. A tourist, oppressed at the sight of these living debris, swooned from emotion. The merchant from Neuchatel perseveres for two days, bandaging wounds and writing for the dying letters of farewell to their families. We are obliged to quiet the compassionate excitement of a Belgian, fearing that he will have an attack of burning fever.

Some men of the detachment, left to garrison the city, try to help their comrades, but cannot endure the sight which breaks down their courage, striking too keenly upon their

34

imagination. Nevertheless, a corporal of the engineer corps, wounded at Magenta, almost restored to health and about to return to his battalion, but whose orders leave him a few days of liberty, aids us with courage and perseverance.

The French Commissary, remaining in Castiglione, finally grants, on my insistence, authority to utilize for service in the hospitals, some healthy prisoners, and three or four Austrian physicians who aid the efforts of the few surgeons left in Castiglione.

A German physician remaining voluntarily on the battle-field to care for the soldiers, dedicates himself to the injured of both armies. After three days the Commissary sends him back to Mantua to rejoin his compatriots.

"Do not leave me to die," exclaim some of these agonized men seizing my hand in despair, but their death is not long delayed.

"Ah, sir, if you would write to my father, that he might console my poor mother!" said to me, with tears in his eyes, a corporal named Mazuet, scarcely twenty years old. I noted down the address of his parents and a few minutes later he had ceased to live. The parents, who dwelt on rue d' Alger, in Lyons, and of whom this young man, enlisted as a volunteer, was the only son, received no other information about their child than that which I sent to them. He very probably, like so many others, has been enscribed, "disappeared."

An old sergeant, decorated with many chevrons, repeated with profound melancholy and an air of conviction full of bitterness: "If some one had cared for me sooner, I should have lived, whereas, this evening I will die." That evening he died.

"I do not want to die! I do not want to die!" cries, with savage energy, a grenadier of the guard, full of strength and health three days before, but who, mortally wounded, and feeling sure that his minutes are irrevocably numbered, fights against this dark certainty. I talk to him, he listens to me, and this man, calmed, soothed, consoled, finally resigns himself to die with the simplicity of a child.

In the back of the church, on the steps of an altar, a Chasseur d' Afrique lies on straw. Three balls have struck him, one on the right side, one on the left shoulder, the third remained in the right leg. It is Sunday, and he asserts that he has eaten nothing since Friday. He is covered with dried mud flecked with blood, his clothing is torn; his shirt is in tatters. After I had washed his wounds, given him a little bouillon and wrapped him in covers, he put my hand to his lips with an expression of unspeakable gratitude. Later we were able to send him to a better hospital.

At the entrance of the church is a Hungarian who cries unceasingly, calling in heartrending tones for a physician. His back and his shoulders, ploughed with grapeshot, appear as if torn by iron hooks and are one mass of quivering, raw flesh. The rest of his body is swollen, green and black—horrible. He can neither lie down nor sit up. I dip some packages of lint in cool water and try to make a cushion for him, but gangrene soon carries him off.

A little further on lies a dying Zouave who is weeping bitter tears, and we console him as if he were a little child. The preceding fatigue, the lack of food and repose, the intensity of the pain, the fear of dying without help, excites even in these brave soldiers a nervous sensibility which betrays itself by sobs. One of their chief thoughts, when they are not suffering too cruelly, is the memory of their mother, and the fear of the grief she will experience on learning of their fate. On the corpse of a soldier we found, hanging from his neck, a medallion containing the portrait of an aged woman, without doubt his mother, which with his left hand he was pressing on his heart.

In the part nearest the great door of the church Maggiore lie, now, on straw, enveloped in covers, about a hundred French noncommissioned officers and soldiers. They are ranged in two nearly parallel ranks, between which one can pass. Their wounds have been dressed. The distribution of soup has taken place. They are quiet. They follow me with their eyes; all heads turn to the left if I go to the left, to the right when I go to the right. Sincere thanks are visible on their astonished faces. "One can easily see that he is a Parisian," say some. "No," retort others, "he seems to be a Southerner." "Truly, sir, are you not from Bordeaux?" asks a third, and each wishes that I might be from his city or province. I met afterwards some of these wounded men, who had become crippled invalids. Recognizing me, they stopped to express their gratitude because I had nursed them in Castiglione. "We called you 'the gentleman in white,'" said one, in his picturesque language, "for you were always dressed entirely in white. It is true the weather did not fail to be hot."

The resignation of the poor soldiers was often touching; they suffered without complaint, they died humbly and silently.

On the other side of the church, some wounded Austrian prisoners fear to receive care which they distrust. They angrily tear off their bandages, opening their bleeding wounds. Others remain silent, dejected, impassive. But the greater number are far from being insensible to kindness and their faces express their thanks. One of them, about nineteen years of age, who with forty of his compatriots is pushed into the deep recesses of the church, has been without food for two days. He has lost one eye, he trembles with fever, he is scarcely able to speak or to drink a little bouillon. Our nursing revives him; twenty-four hours later when we are able to send him to Brescia, he leaves us with sorrow, almost with despair, pressing to his lips the hands of the good-hearted women of Castiglione, whom he entreats not to abandon him.

Another prisoner, a prey to a burning fever, draws attention to himself. He is not yet twenty years of age and his hair is already perfectly white; it became white during the battle, as his wounded comrades near whom he lies assure us.

The women of Castiglione, seeing that I make no distinction in nationality, imitate my example, showing the same kindness to all these men of such different origin and who are to them all equally strangers. "Tutti Fratelli," they repeat with compassion. "All are brothers."

Honor to these compassionate women, to these young girls of Castiglione! As devoted as they are modest, they give way neither before fatigue, nor disgust, nor sacrifice; nothing repels, wearies or disheartens them.

For the soldier recommencing the every-day life of the campaign, after the fatigue and emotions of a battle like that of Solferino, the memories of his family become more strong than ever. That mental state is vividly described by the following lines from an officer writing from Volta to his brother in France:

"You cannot imagine how the soldiers are moved when they catch sight of the baggage-master who distributes the letters to the army; because he brings to us, understand, news from France, from our native land, from our parents, from our friends. Each one listens, watches, and stretches to him eager hands. The happy men, who receive a letter—open it hurriedly and devour it immediately; the rest, deprived of this happiness, depart with heavy heart and isolate themselves in order to think about those so far away.

"Sometimes a name is called to which there is no response. The men glance at each other, they question among themselves, they wait. 'Dead,' murmurs a voice, and the baggage-master files the letter away and returns it unopened to the writer. They had rejoiced when they sent it, and had said to one another. 'He will be happy to receive it!' When they see it returned, their poor hearts will break."

The streets of Castiglione are quieter; the deaths and the departures have left vacancies.

In spite of the arrival of new wagons full of wounded, order, little by little, is established and regular attendance commences.

The convoys from Castiglione to Brescia are more frequent. They consist principally of hospital wagons and heavy carts which, constantly carrying, to the French Commissary Department, gun supplies, and provisions, go back empty to Brescia.

They are drawn by oxen, walking slowly under the fierce sun and through the thick dust in which the pedestrian sinks to his ankles. These uncomfortable wagons are covered with branches of trees which very imperfectly protect from the rays of the coming sun. The wounded, piled up, one may say, one upon another. It is difficult to imagine the torments of this long ride.

In these wagons some groan, others call for their mother; there are the ravings and delirium of fever, sometimes curses and blasphemies.

The least interest shown to these unhappy men, a kind salutation, gives them pleasure and they return it at once with expressions of gratitude.

In all the villages along the road leading to Brescia, the women sitting before their doors, silently prepare lint. The Communal authorities have had prepared, drinks, bread and nourishment. When a convoy arrives the women of the village go to the wagons, wash the wounds, renew the lint compresses, which they moisten with fresh water. They pour spoonfuls of bouillon, wine or lemonade in the mouths of those who have not the strength to raise their heads or extend their arms.

In Montechiaro, three small hospitals are under the care of the women of the people, who nurse with as much wisdom as kindheartedness. In Guidizzolo, about one thousand invalids are placed in a large castle. In Volta, some hundreds of Austrians are received in an old monastery which has been transformed into barracks. In Cavriana, they establish in the church a number of Hungarians who had been forty-eight hours without help. In the field-hospital of the headquarters, chloroform is used in operating; this produces, in the Austrians, almost immediate insensibility, and in the French nervous contractions, accompanied by exaltation before unconsciousness results.

The people of Cavriana are entirely without provisions; the soldiers of the guard feed them by sharing with them their rations and their mess; the country has been laid waste, and almost everything edible, cattle, garden produce, etc., has been sold to the Austrian troops. The French army has campaign food in abundance, but only with difficulty can it procure the butter, meat and vegetables necessary for the ordinary food of soldiers.

The wounded of the Sardinian army, who have been transported to Desenzano, Rivoltella, Lonato, and Pozzolenzo, are in conditions less disadvantageous than the French and Austrians temporarily established in

Castiglione—Desenzano and Rivoltella not having been occupied at a few days interval by two different armies. Food is still to be found there; the hospitals are better kept and the inhabitants, less troubled, actively support the nursing service. The sick are sent to Brescia in good carts provided with thick beds of hay. They are protected from the sun by arches of interlaced foliage which support a strong linen cover.

The feeling that one has of his own insufficiency in such solemn circumstances, is an inexpressible suffering. It is extremely painful to feel that you cannot help all those who lie before you, because of their great number, or aid those who appeal to you with supplications. Long hours pass before you reach the most unfortunate. You are stopped by one, petitioned by another, all equally worthy of pity. Embarrassed at each step by the multitude of miserable sufferers who press about you, who surround you, who beg support and help. Then, why turn to the left, while on the right are so many men who will soon die without a word of consolation, without even a single glass of water to appease their burning thirst? The thought of the importance of one human life that one might be able to save; the desire to alleviate

44

the tortures of so many unfortunate and to restore their courage, the forced and unceasing activity which one imposes on himself in such moments, gives a supreme energy, a thirst to carry help to the greatest number possible. One becomes no longer moved by the thousand scenes of this terrible tragedy, one passes, with indifference, before the most hideously disfigured corpses and glances almost coldly at sights, so much more horrible than those already described, that the pen refuses absolutely to depict them; but it happens, sometimes, that the heart suddenly breaks, struck all at once by a poignant sadness at the sight of a single incident, an isolated fact, an unexpected detail, which goes directly to the soul, draws out our sympathy, moves the most impressionable cords of our being and brings a realization of the whole horror of this tragedy.

Worn out with fatigue, but unable to sleep, I have my little carriage harnessed on the afternoon of Monday, the twenty-seventh, and go away about 6 o'clock to breathe in the open air the freshness of the evening and to find a little repose by escaping, for a moment, from the dismal sights which surround me on every side in Castiglione.

It was a favorable time, for no movement

of the troops had been ordered during the day.

Calm had succeeded the terrible agitation of the previous days. Here and there are visible pools of dried blood which redden the battlefield. One meets newly turned earth, white with freshly strewn lime, indicating the place where repose the victims of the twenty-fourth.

At Solferino, whose square tower has proudly dominated for some centuries that country, where for the third time have just met two of the greatest powers of modern days, one still picks up much debris which covers, even in the cemeteries, the crosses and the bloody stones of the tombs. The ground is strewn with swords, guns, haver-sacks, cartridge boxes, tin boxes, shakos, hel-mets and belts. Almost everything is twisted, torn and broken.

I arrive at Cavriana at about 9 o'clock in the evening.

The train of war surrounding the head-quarters of the Emperor of France is an imposing sight.

I seek the Marshal, Duke of Magenta, with whom I am personally acquainted.

Not knowing exactly where his army corps is encamped, I stop my little carriage on the park opposite the house occupied, since Friday evening, by the Emperor Napoleon. I find myself suddenly in the midst of a group of generals, sitting on straw chairs and wooden stools, smoking their cigars and inhaling the fresh air before the improvised palace of the Sovereign.

While I inquire about the location of Marshal MacMahon, several generals, very suspicious of my arrival, question the corporal, wounded at Magenta, who begged permission to accompany me on this excursion through the armies as his rank would ensure me safe conduct. Sitting beside the coachman, he gives me, in a certain degree, official character. The generals desire to know who I am and to discover the object of the mission with which they suppose I am charged, for they cannot imagine that a simple traveler would dare to risk himself alone in the midst of the camps at such a time.

The corporal, who knows nothing, remains impenetrable, while he replies respectfully to their questions. Their curiosity increases considerably when they see me leave for Borghetto where the Duke of Magenta is.

The second corps, commanded by the Marshal, has been moved from Cavriana to Castellaro, which is at a distance of five kilometers; its divisions are encamped on the right and left of the road leading from Castellaro to Monzambano. The Marshal, himself, with his staff, occupies Borghetto.

Although the night has arrived, we continue our way. The fires of the bivouac, fed by whole trees, and the lighted tents of the officers, present a picturesque appearance. The last murmurings of a sleeping, yet watchful, camp soothes a little my excited imagination. Under this beautiful star-lit sky, a solemn silence at last takes the place of the noises and emotions of the preceding days. I breathe with delight the pure sweet air of a splendid Italian night.

Having obtained only incomplete information, we mistake our way and follow a road leading to Volta. We are about to fall into the army corps of General Neil, made Marshal three days before, which is encamped on the outskirts of the town.

My Italian coachman is so frightened at the idea of being very near the Austrian lines that, more than once, I am obliged to take the reins from his hands and give them to the corporal seated beside him on the box. The poor man had run away from Mantua several days before to save himself from the Austrian service, taking refuge in Brescia, he hired out as a coachman. His fears grow greater on hearing the discharge of a distant gun, fired by some one who disappears in the underbrush. After the retreat of the Austrian army, many of the deserters hid themselves in the cellars of the houses of the villages, abandoned by their owners and partially plundered. In order not to be captured, they, at first, ate and drank in those underground retreats, then, being at the end of their resources and pressed by hunger, but well armed, they ventured out at night.

The unhappy and terrified Mantuan can no longer guide his horse. He constantly turns his head, he casts affrighted glances at all the thickets along the road, at all the hedges and hovels, fearing, any moment, to see emerge some hidden Austrians.

His fears increase at every turn of the road and he almost swoons, when, in the silence of the night we are surprised with a shot from a guard, whom we do not see on account of the darkness. His terror knows no limit when we almost collide with a large, wide open umbrella which we vaguely catch sight of at the side of the road near a path leading to Volta. That poor umbrella, riddled with bullets and balls was, probably, a part of the baggage of some canteen-woman who had lost it during the storm of the twenty-fourth.

We were retracing the road to reach Borghetto. It was after 11 o'clock. We were making the horse gallop and our modest vehicle rolled across the space, almost without noise, on to the Strato Cavallara, when cries of "Who goes there? Who goes there? Who goes there? or I fire," came like a bolt from the mouth of an invisible sentinel. "France," replies immediately a loud voice, which adds, in giving his rank: "Corporal in the First Engineer Corps, Company Seventh." "Go on," is the reply. Without this presence of mind of the corporal we would have received a shot almost in the face.

Finally, at a quarter before twelve we reach, without other adventure, the first houses of Borghetto.

All is dark and silent. However, a light shines on the ground floor of a house on the principal street, where are at work in a low room the accounting officers. Although embarrassed in their work and very much astonished at our appearance at such an hour, they treat us very kindly. A paymaster, Signor Outrey, gives me a cordial invitation to be his guest. His orderly brings a mattress on which I throw myself, completely dressed, to rest for several hours, after drinking some excellent bouillon, which seems to me the more delicious as I am hungry and for several days have eaten nothing even passable. I can sleep quietly, not being, as in Castiglione, suffocated with fetid exhalations and tormented with the flies, which though satiated with corpses, attack also the living.

The corporal and the driver settled themselves simply in the carriage, remaining in the street, but the unfortunate Mantuan, always in great terror, could not shut his eyes during the whole night and the next day he was more dead than alive.

Tuesday, the twenty-eighth, at six in the morning I was received most kindly by Marshal MacMahon. At ten o'clock I was on the way to Cavriana. Soon after I entered the modest house, since historic, for there was lodged the Emperor Napoleon.

At three o'clock in the afternoon I found myself once more in the midst of the wounded of Castiglione, who expressed their joy at seeing me again.

The thirtieth of June I was in Brescia.

This city, so charming and picturesque, is transformed, not into a large temporary shelter for the wounded like Castiglione, but into a vast hospital. Its two cathedrals, its palaces, its churches, its monasteries, its colleges, its barracks, in a word all its buildings receive the victims of Solferino.

Fifteen thousand beds, of some sort, have been improvised in forty-eight hours. The inhabitants have done more than was ever done before under similar circumstances.

In the centre of the city the old basilica, "il Duomo recchio," contains a thousand wounded. The people come to them in crowds, women of every class bring them quantities of oranges, jellies, biscuits and delicacies. The humblest widow or the poorest little old woman believes that she must present her tribute of sympathy and her modest offering.

Similar scenes occur in the new cathedral, a magnificent temple of white marble, where the wounded are taken by the hundreds. It is the same in forty other buildings, churches or hospitals which contain nearly twenty thousand wounded.

The municipality of Brescia understood the extraordinary duty imposed upon it by such grave circumstances. With a permanent existence it associates with itself the best men of the town, who bring to it eager co-operation.

In opening a monastery, a school, a church, the municipality created, in a few hours, as if by magic, hospitals with hundreds of beds, vast kitchens, improvised laundries for linen and everything that would be necessary.

These measures were taken with so much courage that, after a few days, one was able to admire the good order and regular management of these hurriedly arranged hospitals. The population of Brescia, which was forty thousand, was suddenly almost doubled by the great number of wounded and sick. The physicians, numbering one hundred and forty, displayed great self-devotion during the whole duration of their fatiguing service. They were helped by the medical students and some volunteers. Aid committees being organized, a special commission was appointed to receive donations of bedding, linen and provisions of all kinds; another commission administered the depot or central store house.

In the large rooms of the hospitals, the officers are ordinarily separated from the soldiers. The Austrians are not mixed with the allies. The series of beds are all alike, on the shelf above the bed of each soldier, his uniform and military cap indicate to which branch of the service he belongs.

They have commenced to refuse permission for the crowd to enter, it embarrasses and hinders the nurses.

At the side of soldiers, with resigned faces, are others who murmur and complain. The idea of an amputation scarcely frightens the French soldier, because of his careless nature, but he is impatient and irritable; the Austrian, of a less thoughtless disposition, is more inclined to be melancholy in his isolation.

I find in these hospital wards some of our wounded from Castiglione. They are better cared for now, but their torments are not ended.

Here, is one of the heroes of the Imperial Flying Guard, wounded at Solferino. Shot in the leg, he passed several days at Castiglione, where I dressed his wounds for the first time. He is stretched on a straw mattress; the expression of his face denotes profound suffering; his eyes are hollow and shining; his great pallor gives evidence that purulent fever has set in to complicate and increase the gravity of his condition; his lips are dry; his voice trembles; the assurance of the brave man has given place to fear and timidity; care even unnerves him; he is afraid to have any one approach his poor injured leg which the gangrene has already attacked.

A French surgeon, who makes the amputations, passes by his bed; the sick man, whose touch is like burning iron, seizes his hand and presses it in his own.

"Do not hurt me! My suffering is terrible!" he cries.

But one must act, and without delay. Twenty other wounded must be operated on during the same morning, and one hundred and fifty are waiting for bandages. One has not time to pity a single case nor to await the end of his hesitation. The surgeon, cool and resolute, replies: "Let me do it." Then he rapidly lifts the covering. The broken leg is swollen double its natural size; from three places flows a quantity of fetid pus, purple stains prove that as an artery has been broken, the sole remedy, if there is one, is amputation.

Amputation! Terrible word for this poor young man, who sees before him no other alternative than an immediate death or the miserable life of a cripple.

He has no time to prepare himself for the last decision, and trembling with anguish, he cries out in despair: "Oh! What are you going to do?" The surgeon does not reply.

"Nurse, carry him away, make haste!" he says. But a heartrending cry bursts from that panting breast; the unskilled nurse has seized the motionless, yet sensitive, leg much too near the wound; the broken bones penetrating the flesh, has caused new torments to the soldier whose hanging leg shakes with the jolts of the transportation to the operating room.

Fearful procession! It seems as if one were leading a victim to death.

He lies finally on the operating table. Nearby, on another table, a linen covers the instruments. The surgeon, occupied with his work, hears and sees only his operation. A young army doctor holds the arms of the patient, while the nurse seizes the healthy leg and draws the invalid to the edge of the table. At this the frightened man shrieks: "Do not let me fall!" and he seizes convulsively in his arms the young physician, ready to support him and who pale from emotion is himself almost equally distressed.

The operator, one knee on the floor and his hand armed with the terrible knife, places his arm about the gangrenous limb and cuts the skin all around. A piercing cry sounds through the hospital. The young physician, face to face, with the tormented man can see on his contracted features every detail of his atrocious agony.

"Courage," he says, in a low tone to the soldier, whose hands he feels gripping his back, "two minutes more and you will be saved."

The doctor stands up again; he separates the skin from the muscles which it covers, leaving them bare; as he draws back the skin he cuts away the flesh, then returning to the attack, with a vigorous turn, he cuts away every muscle to the bone; a torrent of blood gushes out of the arteries, just opened, covering the operator and flowing down on to the floor.

Calm and expressionless, the rough operator does not speak a word; but, suddenly, in the midst of the silence reigning in the room, he turns in anger to the awkward nurse, reproaching him for not knowing how to press on the arteries. This latter, inexperienced, did not know how to prevent the hemorrhage by applying his thumb properly on the bleeding arteries.

The wounded man, overcome by suffering, articulates feebly, "Oh! it is enough, let me die!" and a cold sweat runs down his face.

But he must bear it still another minute,— a minute which seems an eternity.

57

The young physician, ever full of sympathy, counts the seconds as he watches sometimes the operating surgeon, sometimes the patient, whose courage he tries to sustain, saying to him: "Only one minute more!"

Indeed, the moment for the saw has come and already one hears the grinding of the steel as it penetrates the living bone, separating from the body the member half gangrenous.

But the pain has been too great for that weak, exhausted body; the groans have ceased, for the sick man has swooned. The surgeon, who is no longer guided by his cries and his groans, fearing that this silence may be that of death, looks at him uneasily to assure himself that he has not expired.

The restoratives, held in reserve, succeed, with difficulty, in reviving his dull, half-closed, vacant eyes. The dying man, however, seems to return to life, he is weak and shattered, but at least his greatest sufferings are over.

Imagine such an operation on an Austrian, understanding neither Italian nor French and letting himself be led like a sheep or an ox to slaughter without being able to exchange one word with his well-meaning tormentors! The French meet everywhere with sympathy; they are flattered, pampered, encouraged; when one speaks to them about the battle of Solferino, they brighten up and discuss it: That memory, full of glory for them; drawing their thoughts elsewhere than on themselves, lessens a little their unhappiness. But the Austrians have not this good fortune. In the hospitals where they are crowded, I insist upon seeing them and almost by force enter their rooms. With what gratitude these good men welcome my words of consolation and the gift of a little tobacco! On their resigned faces is depicted a lively gratitude, which they do not know how to express. Their looks tell more than any word of thanks.

Some of them possess two or three paper florins, a small fortune for them, but they cannot change this modest value for coins.

The officers particularly show hearty appreciation of the attentions bestowed upon them. In the hospital where he is lodged, Prince von Isenburg occupies with another German prince, a comfortable little room.

During several successive days I distribute, without distinction of nationality, tobacco, pipes and cigars in the churches and hospitals where the odor of the tobacco lessens a little the nauseous stench produced by the crowding of so many patients in suffocating places. Besides that, it is a distraction, a means of dispelling the fears of the wounded before the amputation of a member; not a few are operated on with a pipe in the mouth, and some die smoking.

Finally all the supply of tobacco in Brescia is exhausted. It must be brought from Milan.

An eminent inhabitant of Brescia, Signor Carlo Borghetti, takes me in his carriage, from hospital to hospital. He helps me to distribute my modest gifts of tobacco, arranged by the merchants in thousands of little bags that are carried by willing soldiers in very large baskets.

Everywhere I am well received. Only a doctor of Lombardy, named Calini, will not allow the distribution of cigars in the hospital San Luca, which is confided to his care. In other places the physicians, on the contrary, show themselves almost as grateful as their patients. But wishing to try once more at San Luca, I visit again that hospital and succeed in making a large distribution of cigars, to the great joy the poor wounded, whom I had innocently made suffer the torments of Tantalus.

During the course of my investigations I

penetrate into a series of rooms forming the second floor of a large monastery, a kind of labyrinth of which the ground and the first floors are full of the sick. I find in one of the upper rooms four or five wounded and feverish patients, in another ten or fifteen, in a third about twenty, all neglected (this is very excusable; there were so many wounded, everywhere), complaining bitterly of not having seen a nurse for several hours and begging insistently that some one bring them bouillon in place of cold water which they have for their only drink. At the end of an interminable corridor, in a little isolated room, is dying absolutely alone, motionless on a mattress, a young corporal attacked with tetanus. Although he seems full of life as his eyes are wide open, he hears and understands nothing and remains neglected.

Many of the soldiers beg me to write to their relatives, some to their captains, who replace in their eyes their absent families.

In the hospital of Saint Clement, a lady of Brescia, Countess Bronna, occupies herself, with saintly self-abnegation, in nursing those who have had limbs amputated. The French soldiers speak of her with enthusiasm, the most repellant details do not stop her. "Sono madre!" she says to me with

61

simplicity: "I am a mother!" These words well express her devotion as complete as motherly.

In the hospital San Gaetano, a Franciscan monk, distinguishes himself by his zeal and kindness to the sick. A convalescent Piedmontese, speaking French and Italian, translates the petitions of the French soldiers to the Lombardy physicians. They keep him as interpreter.

In a neighboring hospital chloroform is used. Some patients are chloroformed with difficulty, accidents result and sometimes it is in vain that they try to revive a man who a few minutes before was speaking.

I am stopped many times on the street by kind people who beg me to come to their homes, for a minute, to act as interpreter to the wounded French officers, lodged in their houses, surrounded by the best care, but whose language they do not understand. The invalids, excited and uneasy, are irritated at not being understood, to the great distress of the family whose sympathetic kindness is received with the bad humour that fever and suffering often call forth. One of them, whom an Italian physician desires to bleed, imagining that they wish to amputate him, resists with all his strength, overheating himself and doing himself much harm. A few words of explanation in their mother tongue, in the midst of this lamentable confusion, alone succeed in calming and tranquilizing these invalids of Solferino.

With what patience the inhabitants of Brescia devote themselves to these who have sacrificed themselves in order to deliver them from a foreign rule! They feel a real grief when their charge dies. These adopted families religiously follow to the cemetery, accompanying to its last resting place, the coffin of the French officer, their guest of a few days, for whom they weep as for a friend, a relative or a son, but whose name, perhaps, they do not know.

During the night the soldiers, who have died in the hospitals, are interred. Their names and numbers are noted down, which was rarely done in Castiglione. For example, the parents of Corporal Mazuet, aided by me in the Chiesa Maggiore and who lived in Lyons, 3 Rue d'Alger, never received other information about their son than that which I sent them.

All the cities of Lombardy considered it due to their honor to share in the distribution of the wounded.

In Bergamo and Cremona special commissions organized in haste are aided by auxillary committees of devoted ladies. In one of the hospitals of Cremona an Italian physician having said: "We keep the good things for our friends of the allied army, but we give to our enemies only what is absolutely necessary, and if they die, so much the worse for them!" A lady, directing one of the hospitals of that city, hastened to disapprove of these barbarous words, saying that she always took the same care of Austrians, French and Sardinians, not wishing to make any difference between friends and enemies, "for," she said, "Our Lord Jesus Christ made no distinction between men when it was a question of doing them good."

In Cremona, as everywhere else, the French physicians regret their insufficient number. "I cannot, without profound sorrow," said Dr. Sonrier, "think of a small room of twenty-five beds assigned, in Cremona, to the most dangerously wounded Austrians. I see again their faces, emaciated and wan, with complexion pallid from exhaustion and blood poisoning, begging with heartrending gestures, accompanied by pitiful cries, for one last favor, the amputation of a limb (which they had hoped to save), to end an intolerable agony of which we are forced to remain powerless spectators."

Besides the group of courageous and indefatigable surgeons, whose names I would like to be able to cite (for, certainly, if to kill men is a title to glory, to nurse them and cure them, often at the risk of one's own life, merits indeed esteem and gratitude), medical students hasten from Bologna, Pisa and other Italian cities. A Canadian surgeon, Dr. Norman Bettun, professor of anatomy in Toronto, comes to assist these devoted men. Besides the people of Lombardy, French, Swiss and Belgian tourists seek to render themselves useful, but their efforts had to be limited to the distribution of oranges, ices, coffee, lemonade and tobacco.

In Plaisance, whose three hospitals are administered by private individuals, and by ladies serving as nurses, one of these last, a young lady, supplicated by her family to renounce her intention to pass her days in the hospital, on account of the contagious fevers there, continued her labors so willingly and with such kindness that she was greatly esteemed by all the soldiers. "She enlivens the hospital," they said.

How valuable, in the cities of Lombardy, would have been some hundreds of voluntary nurses, devoted, experienced and, above all, previously instructed! They would have rallied around themselves the meagre band of assistants and the scattered forces. Not only was time lacking to those who were capable of counselling and guiding; but the necessary knowledge and experience was not possessed by the greater number of those who could offer only personal devotion, which was insufficient and often useless. What, indeed, in spite of their good will, could a handful of persons do in such urgent need? After some weeks the compassionate enthusiasm began to cool and the people, as inexperienced as they were injudicious in their kindness, sometimes brought improper food to the wounded, so that it was necessary to deny them entrance to the churches and hospitals.

Many persons, who would have consented to pass one or two hours a day with the sick, gave up their intention, because a special permission was necessary, which could only be obtained by petitioning the authorities. Strangers disposed to help met with all kinds of unexpected hindrances, of a nature to discourage them. But voluntary hospital workers, well chosen and capable, sent by societies with the sanction of the governments and respected because of an agreement between the belligerents, would have surmounted the difficulties and done incomparably more good.

During the first eight days after the battle the wounded, of whom the physicians said, in low tones, when passing by their beds and shaking their heads: "There is nothing more to be done," received no more attention and died neglected. And is not this very natural when the scarcity of the nurses is compared with the enormous number of the wounded? An inexorable and cruel logic insists that these unfortunate men should be left to perish without further care and without having given to them the precious time that must be reserved for the soldiers who could be cured. They were numerous, however, and not deaf, those unfortunate men on whom was passed such pitiless judgment! Soon they perceive their deserted condition and with a broken and embittered heart gasp out the last breath while no one notices.

The death of many a one among them is rendered more sad and bitter by the proximity, on a cot by his side, of a young soldier, slightly wounded, whose foolish jokes leave him neither peace nor tranquillity. On the other side, one of his companions in misery has just died; and, he dying, must see and hear the funeral ceremony, much too rapidly performed, which shows him in advance his own. Finally, about to die, he sees men, profiting by his weakness, search his knapsack and steal what they desire.

For that dying man there have been, lying in the postoffice for eight days, letters from his family; if he could have had them, they would have been to him a great consolation; he has entreated the nurses to bring them that he may read them before his last hour, but they replied unkindly, that they had not time as there was so much else to do.

Better would it have been for you, poor martyr, if you had perished, struck dead on the field of butchery, in the midst of the splendid abomination which men call "Glory!" Your name, at least, would not have been forgotten, if you had fallen near your colonel defending the flag of your regiment. It would almost have been better for you had you been buried alive by the peasants commissioned for that purpose, when you, unconscious, were carried from the hill of the Cypresses, from the foot of the tower of Solferino or from the plains of Medole. Your agony would not have been long. Now, it is a succession of miseries that you must endure, it is no longer the field of honor that is presented to you, but cold death with all its terrors, and the word "disappeared" for a funeral oration.

What has become of the love of glory which electrified this brave soldier at the commencement of the campaign and during that day at Solferino, when, risking his own life, he so courageously attempted to take the lives of his fellow-creatures, whose blood he ran, with such light feet, to shed? Where is the irresistible allurement? Where the contagious enthusiasm, increased by the odor of powder, by the flourish of trumpets and by the sound of military music, by the noise of cannon and the whistling of bullets which hide the view of danger, suffering and death.

In these many hospitals of Lombardy may be seen at what price is bought that which men so proudly call "Glory," and how dearly this glory costs.

The battle of Solferino is the only one during our century to be compared by the magnitude of its losses with the battles of Moscow, Leipzig and Waterloo.

As a consequence of the twenty-fourth of June, 1859, it has been calculated that there were in killed and wounded, in the Austrian and Franco-Sardinian Armies, three field-marshals, nine generals, fifteen hundred and sixty-six officers of all grades, of whom six hundred and thirty were Austrians and nine hundred and thirty-six allies, and about forty thousand soldiers and non-commissioned officers.

Besides that, from the fifteenth of June to the thirty-first of August, there were in the hospitals of Brescia, according to the official statistics, nineteen thousand six hundred and sixty-five patients with fever and other illnesses, of whom more than nineteen thousand belonged to the Franco-Sardinian Army.

On their side, the Austrians had at least twenty thousand sick soldiers in Venice, beside ten thousand wounded, who, after Solferino, were sent to Verona, where the overcrowded hospitals were finally attacked by gangrene and typhus fever.

Consequently, to the forty thousand killed and wounded on the twenty-fourth of June, must be added more than forty thousand sick with fever or dying from illness caused by the excessive fatigue experienced on the day of the battle or during the days which preceded and succeeded it or from the pernicious effects of the tropical temperature of the plains of Lombardy, or, finally, from the imprudence of these soldiers themselves.

If one does not consider the military point of view, the battle of Solferino was then, from the point of humanity a European catastrophe.

The transportation of the wounded from Brescia to Milan, which takes place during the night because of the torrid heat of the day, presents a dramatic sight with its trains loaded with crippled soldiers arriving at the station filled with crowds of people.

Lighted by the pale flare of the tar torches, the mass of men seems to hold its breath to listen to the groans and the stifled complaints which reach their ears.

The Austrians, in their retreat, having torn up several places on the railroad between Milan and Brescia—this road was restored for use by the first days of July, for the transportation of ammunitions, of supplies and of food sent to the allied army—the evacuation of the hospitals in Brescia was in this way facilitated.

At each station, long and narrow sheds have been constructed to receive the wounded. These, when taken from the cars, are placed on mattresses, arranged in a line one after the other. Under these sheds are set up tables covered with bread, soup, lemonade, wine, water, lint, linen and bandages.

Torches, carried by the young men of the place where the convoy stops, light the darkness. The citizens of Lombardy hasten to present their tribute of gratitude to the conquerors of Solferino; in respectful silence they bandage the wounded whom they have lifted carefully out of the cars to place them on the beds made ready for their use. The women of the country offer refreshing drinks, and food of all kinds, which they distribute on the cars to those who must go on to Milan.

In this city, where about a thousand wounded have arrived every night for several nights in succession, the martyrs of Solferino are received with great kindness. No longer are rose leaves scattered from the flag-ornamented balconies of the luxurious palaces of the Milanese aristocracy, on shining epaulets and on striped gold and enameled orders, by beautiful and graceful ladies whom exaltation and enthusiasm rendered still more beautiful. To-day, in their gratitude, they shed tears of compassion which are interpreted by devotion and sacrifice.

Every family possessing a carriage, goes to the station to transport the wounded. The number of equipages sent by the people of Milan probably exceeds five hundred. The finest carriages as well as the most modest carts are sent every evening to Porto Tosca, where stands the railroad station for Venice. The Italian ladies consider it an honor to themselves to place in their rich carriages, which they have provided with mattresses, sheets and pillows, the guests assigned to them and who are accompanied by the greatest noblemen of Lombardy, aided in this work by their not less considerate servants.

The people applaud the passage of these men, famed because of their suffering. They respectfully uncover their heads. They follow the slow march of the convoy with torches illuminating the sad faces of the wounded, who try to smile. They accompany them to the door of the hospitable palace, where awaits them the most devoted care.

Every family wishes to receive the French wounded and, by all sorts of kindness, try to lessen the sadness caused by distance from home, from parents and from friends.

But after a few days the greater number of the inhabitants of Milan are obliged to remove to the hospitals the wounded whom they have received in their houses. The administration desires to avoid too great scattering of the nursing and any increase of fatigue for the physicians. Before Solferino, the hospitals of this city contained about nine thousand wounded from preceding battles.

Great Milanese ladies watch beside the bed of the simple soldier, of whom they become the guardian angels. Countess Verri, née Borroméo, Madame Uboldi de Capei, Madame Boselli, Madame Sala-Taverna, Countess Taverna and many others, forgetting their luxurious habits, pass whole months by these beds of suffering. Some of these ladies are mothers, whose mourning garments testify to a recent and sorrowful loss. One of them said: "The war robbed me of my oldest son; he died eight months ago, from a shot received while fighting with the French Army at Sebastopol. When I knew that the French wounded were coming to Milan and that I could nurse them, I felt that God was sending me His first consolation."

Countess Verri-Borroméo, president of the Central Aid Committee, has charge of the great depot for linens and lint. In spite of her advanced age she devotes many hours a day to reading to the sick.

All the palaces contain wounded. That of the Borroméo family has received three hundred. The Superior of the Ursulines, Sister

Marina Videmari, has converted her convent into a hospital and serves in it with her companions. This convent-hospital is a model of order and cleanliness.

The Marchioness Pallavicini-Trivulzio, who presides over the great Turin Committee with admirable devotion and self-forgetfulness, collects the donations from different cities and countries; thanks to her activity the depot in Milan, situated contrada San Paolo, remains always well provided.

Some weeks later, in the streets of Milan, there were seen passing a few companies of convalescent French soldiers sadly returning to France. Some have their arms in slings, others are supported by crutches or bear marks of wounds. Their uniforms are well worn and torn, but they wear fine linen, which the rich men of Lombardy have generously given them in exchange for their blood-stained shirts: "Your blood flowed to defend our country," they said, "and we wish to keep these memories of it." These men, not long ago so strong, so robust, now deprived of an arm or a leg or with head bandaged, bear their misfortune with resignation. But, thus incapable of continuing in the army and earning bread for their families, they already with bitterness, behold

75

themselves, after their return to their native land, objects of commiseration and pity, a care to others and to themselves.

In one of the hospitals of Milan, a sergeant of the Zouave Guard, with an energetic and proud face, who has had one leg amputated and had borne that operation without a complaint, was seized, some time after, with extreme sadness, although his health was improving and his recovery rapidly taking place. This sadness, increasing daily, was incomprehensible. A Sister of Charity, perceiving tears in his eyes, questioned so insistently that he at last confessed that he was the sole support of his aged and infirm mother to whom he used to send each month five francs of his pay. He added that, being unable to help her, this poor woman must be in great need of money. The Sister of Charity, touched with compassion, gave him five francs, the value of which was immediately sent to France. When the directress of the hospital wished to make him another gift, he would not accept it, and said to her thankfully: "Keep this money for others who need it more than I; as for my mother, I hope next month to send her her usual allowance, for I count on soon being able to work."

A lady of Milan, bearing an illustrious name, placed at the disposition of the wounded one of her palaces, with one hundred and fifty beds. Among the soldiers, lodged in this magnificent mansion, was a grenadier of the Seventieth Regiment of the French Infantry, who, having undergone an operation, was in danger of death. The lady, trying to console him, spoke to him of his family. He told her that he was the only son of poor peasants in the Department of Gers, and that he was very sad at leaving his parents in misery, for he alone provided for their maintenance. He added that his greatest consolation would be to kiss his mother before he died. Saying nothing to him of her project, the noble lady suddenly decides to leave Milan, takes the train, reaches the Departments of Gers, near the family, whose address she has procured, takes possession of the mother of the wounded man. After having left a large sum of money for the infirm old father, she brings the humble villager with her to Milan; and six days after the confession of the grenadier, the son kisses his mother, weeping and blessing his benefactress.

But why recall so many pitiful and melancholy scenes and thus arouse such painful emotions? Why relate, with complaisance, these lamentable details and dwell upon these distressing pictures?

To this very natural question we reply with another question.

Would it not be possible to establish in every country of Europe, Aid Societies, whose aim would be to provide, during war, volunteer nurses for the wounded, without distinction of nationality?

As they wish us to give up the desires and hopes of the Societies of the Friends of Peace, the beautiful dreams of the Abbot of Saint Pierre and of Count Sellon; as men continue to kill each other without personal enmity, and as the height of glory in war is to exterminate the greatest number possible; as they still dare to say, as did Count Joseph de Maistre, that "war is divine"; as they invent every day with a perseverence worthy of a better aim, instruments of destruction more and more terrible, and as the inventors of these death-dealing engines are encouraged by all the European governments—who arm themselves in emulation one of another—why not profit from a moment of comparative calm and tranquillity in order to settle the question which we have just raised, and which is of such great importance from the double point of view of humanity and Christianity.

Once presented to the consideration of every man, this theme will probably call forth opinions and writings from more competent persons; but, first, must not this idea, presented to the different branches of the great European family, hold the attention and conquer the sympathies of all those who possess an elevated soul and a heart capable of being moved by the suffering of their fellow-men?

Such is the purpose for which this book has been written.

Societies of this kind, once created, with a permanent existence, would be found all ready at the time of war. They should obtain the favor of the authorities of countries where they are created, and beg, in case of war, from the sovereigns of the belligerent powers the permission and the facilities necessary to carry out their purpose. These societies should include in their own and each country, as members of the central committee, the most honorable and esteemed men.

The moment of the commencement of war, the committee would call on those persons who desire to dedicate themselves, for the time being, to this work, which will consist in helping and nursing, under the guidance of experienced physicians, the wounded, first on the battle-field, then in the field and regular hospitals.

Spontaneous devotion is not as rare as one might think. Many persons, sure of being able to do some good, helped and facilitated by a Superior Committee, would certainly go, and others, at their own expense, would undertake a task so essentially beneficent. During our selfish century what an attraction for the generous-hearted and for chivalrous characters to brave the same danger as the soldier with an entirely voluntary mission of peace and consolation.

History proves that it is in no way chimerical to hope for such self-devotion. Two recent facts especially have just confirmed this. They occurred during the war in the East and closely relate to our subject.

While Sisters of Charity were nursing the wounded and sick of the French army in the Crimea, into the Russian and English armies, there came, from the north and west, two groups of self-devoted women nurses.

The Grand Duchess Helen Pavlovna, of Russia, born, Princess Charlotte, of Wurttemberg, widow of the Grand Duke Michael, having enlisted nearly three hundred ladies of St. Petersburg and Moscow, to serve as nurses in the Russian hospitals of the Crimea; she provided them with everything necessary, and these saintly women were blessed by thousands of soldiers.

In England, Miss Florence Nightingale, having received a pressing appeal from Lord Sidney Herbert, Secretary of War of the British Empire, inviting her to go to the aid of the English soldiers in the Orient, this lady did not hesitate to expose herself personally by great self-devotion. In November, 1854, she went to Constantinople and Scutari with thirty-seven English ladies, who, immediately on arrival gave their attention to nursing the great number of men, wounded in the battle of Inkerman. In 1855 Miss Stanley, having come to take part in her labor with fifty new companions, made it possible for Miss Nightingale to go to Balaklava to inspect the hospitals there. The picture of Miss Florence Nightingale, during the night, going through the vast wards of the military hospitals with a small lamp in her hand, noting the condition of each sick man, will never be obliterated from the hearts of the men, who were the objects or the witnesses of her admirable beneficence, and the memory of it will be engraven in history.

Of the multitude of similar good works, ancient or modern, the greater number of which have remained unknown and without fame, how many have been in vain, because they were isolated and were not supported by a united action, which would have wisely joined them together for a common aim.

If voluntary hospital workers could have been found in Castiglione on the twenty-fourth, the twenty-fifth, and the twenty-sixth of June, and also in Brescia, Mantua, and Verona, how much good they might have done.

How many human beings they might have saved from death during that fatal Friday night, when moans and heartrending supplications escaped from the breasts of thousands of the wounded, who were enduring the most acute pains and tormented by the inexpressible suffering of thirst.

If Prince von Isenburg had been rescued sooner, by compassionate hands, from the blood-soaked field on which he was lying unconscious, he would not have been obliged to suffer for several years from wounds aggravated by long neglect; if the sight of his riderless horse had not brought about his discovery among the corpses, he would have perished for lack of help with so many other wounded, who also were creatures of God, and whose death would be equally cruel for their families.

Those good old women, those beautiful young girls of Castiglione could not save the lives of many of those whom they nursed! Besides them were needed experienced men, skillful, decided, previously trained to act with order and harmony, the only means of preventing the accidents, which complicate the wounds and make them mortal.

If there could have been a sufficient number of assistants to remove the wounded quickly from the plains of Medole, from the ravines of San Martin, on the slopes of Mount Fontana, or on the hills of Solferino, there would not have been left during long hours of terrible fear that poor bersaglier, that Uhlan, or that Zouave, who tried to raise himself, in spite of cruel suffering, to gesticulate in vain for some one to send a litter for him. Finally, the risk of burying the living with the dead would have been avoided.

Better means of transportation would have made it possible to avoid in the case of the light infantryman of the Guard the terrible amputation which he had to undergo in Brescia, because of the lack of proper care during the journey from the battle-field to Castiglione.

The sight of those young cripples, deprived of an arm, or a leg, returning sadly to their homes, does it not call forth remorse that there was not more effort made before to avert the evil consequences of the wounds, which, often could have been cured by timely aid?

Would those dead, deserted in the hospitals of Castiglione, or in those of Brescia, many of whom could not make themselves understood, on account of the difference of language, have gasped out their last breath with curses and blasphemies, if they had had near them some compassionate soul to listen to them and console them?

In spite of the official aid, in spite of the zeal of the cities of Lombardy, much remained to be done, although in no other war has been seen so great a display of charity; it was nevertheless unequal to the extent of the help that was needed.

It is not the paid employee, whom disgust drives away, whom fatigue makes unfeeling, unsympathetic and lazy who can fulfil such a noble task. Immediate help is needed, for that which can to-day save the wounded will not save him to-morrow; the loss of time causes gangrene, which leads to death. One must have volunteer nurses, previously trained, accustomed to the work, officially recognized by the commanding officers of the armies, so that they may be facilitated in their mission.

These nurses should not only find their place on the battle-field, but also in the hospitals, where the long weeks pass away painfully for the wounded, without family and without friends. During this short Italian war, there were soldiers who were attacked with home-sickness to such a degree that, without other illness and without wounds, they died. On the other hand, the Italians, and this is comprehensible, showed scarcely any interest in the wounded of the allied army, and still less for the suffering Austrians. It is true, courageous women were found in Italy, whose patience and perseverance never wearied; but, unfortunately, in the end they could be easily counted; the contagious fevers drove many persons away, and the nurses and servants did not respond for any length of time, to that which might have been expected of them. The personnel of the military hospitals is always insufficient; and, if it were doubled or tripled, it would still be insufficient. We must call on the public, it is not possible, it never will be possible to avoid that. Only by this co-operation can one hope to lessen the sufferings of war.

An appeal must be made, a petition presented to the men of all countries, of all classes, to the influential of this world, as well as to the most modest artisan, since all can, in one way or another, each in his own sphere, and according to his strength, co-operate in some measure in this good work.

This appeal is addressed to women as well as to men, to the queen, to the princess seated on the steps of the throne, as well as to the humble orphaned and charitable maid-servant or the poor widow alone in the world, who desires to consecrate her last strength to the good of others.

It is addressed to the general, to the marshal, the Minister of War, as well as to the writer and the man of letters, who, by his publications, can plead with ability for the cause, thereby interesting all mankind, each nation, each country, each family even, since no one can say for certain that he is exempt from the dangers of war.

If an Austrian general and a French general, after having fought one against another at Solferino, could, soon afterwards, finding themselves seated side by side at the hospitable table of the King of Prussia, converse amicably one with the other, what would have prevented them from considering and discussing a question so worthy of their interest and attention?

During the grand manouvers at Cologne, in 1861, King William of Prussia invited to dinner, in Benrath Castle, near Dusseldorf, the officers of the different nations, who were sent there by their governments. Before going to the table the King took by the hand General Forey and General Baumgarten: "Now that you are friends," he said to them, smiling, "sit there, beside one another, and chat." Forey was the victor of Montebello, and Baumgarten was his adversary.

On extraordinary occasions, such as those which assembled at Cologne, at Chalons, or elsewhere, eminent men of the military art of different nations, is it not to be desired that they will profit by this kind of congress to formulate some international, sacred, and accepted principle which, once agreed upon and ratified, would serve as the foundation for societies for aid for the wounded in the different countries of Europe? It is still more important to agree upon and adopt in advance these measures, because when hostilities have commenced, the belligerents are ill-disposed one towards the other, and will not consider these questions, except from the exclusive point of view of their own interests.

Are not small congresses called together of scientists, jurists, medical men, agriculturists, statisticians, and economists, who meet expressly in order to consider questions of much less importance? Are there not international societies which are occupied with questions of charity and public utility? Cannot men, in like manner, meet to solve a problem as important as that of caring for the victims of war?

Humanity and civilization surely demand the accomplishment of such a work. It is a duty, to the fulfilment of which every good man, and every person possessing any influence owes his assistance.

What prince, what ruler, would refuse his support to these societies, and would not be glad to give the soldiers of his army the full assurance that they will be immediately and properly nursed in case they should be wounded?

With permanent societies, such as I propose, the chance of waste and the injudicious distribution of money and supplies would often be avoided. During the war in the East an enormous quantity of lint, prepared by Russian ladies, was sent from St. Petersburg to the Crimea; but the packages, instead of reaching the hospitals to which they were sent, arrived at paper mills which used it all for their own industry.

By perfecting the means of transportation, by preventing the accidents during the journey from the battle-field to the hospital, many amputations will be avoided, and the burden of the governments, which pension the injured will be proportionately lessened.

These societies, by their permanent existence, could also render great service at the time of epidemics, floods, great fires, and other unexpected catastrophies; the humane motive which would have created them would instigate them to act on all occasions in which their labors could be exercised.

This work will necessitate the devotion of a certain number of persons, but it will never lack money in time of war. Each one will bring his offering or his compassion in response to the appeals which will be made by the committee. A nation will not remain indifferent when its children are fighting for its defense. The difficulty is not there; but

the problem rests entirely in the serious preparation, in all countries, of a work of this kind, that is, in the creation of these societies.

In order to establish these committees at the head of the societies, all that is necessary is a little good-will on the part of some honorable and persevering persons. The committees, animated by an international spirit of charity, would create corps of nurses in a latent state, a sort of staff. The committees of the different nations, although independent of one another, will know how to understand and correspond with each other, to convene in congress and, in event of war, to act for the good of all.

If the terrible instruments of destruction now possessed by the nations seem to shorten wars, will not, on the other hand, the battles be more deadly? And in this century, when the unexpected plays such an important role, may not war bring about the most sudden and unforseen results?

Are there not, in these considerations alone, more than sufficient reasons for us not to allow ourselves to be taken unawares?

CPSIA information can be obtained at www.ICGtesting.com
Printed in the USA
BVOW08s1110300714

361049BV00025B/709/P